MAY 1 4 1999

NAPA CITY-COUNTY LIBRARY

3 1128 00751 6133

J

☑ **W9-CQF-378**

On the Trail
of the
Komodo
Dragon

J
590.72

Scientists Probe 11 Animal Mysteries

On the Trail
of the
Komodo Dragon

and Other Explorations of Science in Action

Jack Myers, Ph.D.
Senior Science Editor
HIGHLIGHTS FOR CHILDREN

Illustrated by John Rice

Boyds Mills Press

NAPA CITY-COUNTY LIBRARY
580 COOMBS STREET
NAPA CA 94559-3396

Text and illustrations copyright © 1999 by Boyds Mills Press
All rights reserved

Photo credits: Page 46: Stan L. Lindstedt, Ph.D.; 50: Eric B. Wheeldon, Ph.D.

The illustration on pages 10 and 11 is adapted from *Domestic Animal Behavior for Veterinarians and Animal Scientists* by Katherine A. Houpt, V.M.D., Ph.D., and Thomas R. Wolski, D.V.M., Ames: The Iowa State University Press, 1982.

Published by Caroline House
Boyds Mills Press, Inc.
A Highlights Company
815 Church Street
Honesdale, Pennsylvania 18431
Printed in Mexico

Myers, Jack,
    On the trail of the komodo dragon : and other explorations of science in action /
by Jack Myers, Ph.D. ; illustrated by John Rice.—1st edition.
[64]p. : ill. ; cm.
Includes index and bibliography.
Summary: Intriguing questions about animals answered by scientists in these eleven
explorations taken from the award-winning column in *Highlights for Children* magazine.
ISBN 1-56397-761-3
1. Science—Miscellanea—Juvenile literature. 2. Animals—Miscellanea—Juvenile literature.
3. Questions and answers—Juvenile literature. [1. Science. 2. Animals. 3. Questions and
answers.]
I. Rice, John, ill. II. Title.
591 —dc21 1999 CIP
Library of Congress Catalog Number 98-73073

First edition, 1999
The text of this book is set in 13-point Berkeley.
The illustrations are done in watercolor.

10 9 8 7 6 5 4 3 2 1

CONTENTS

Introduction

Science is the search for understanding of our world. All the fun and excitement of science is in that search. That's where the action is. And that's why we have called this series Science in Action. It tells about the explorations and discoveries as they happened.

All of these explorations have appeared in *Highlights for Children*. Earlier they were called Science Reporting. That also was a good title because each has been based on an original and current report cited on page 61.

Most of these chapters tell about neat, clean scientific work that gave us answers to some great questions of pure curiosity. In some cases, new findings were made since my account was published in *Highlights*. I have updated and revised them as needed.

One chapter in particular, "Talking to Chimpanzees," has been greatly expanded because the first attempt to teach a chimpanzee named Washoe to use human language led to a great debate and to many more studies. I have included what I see as the major steps that came after Washoe. But more will probably come in the future.

This volume is about the living world. It's about animals, their behavior, and their part in nature. Grouping these explorations together is really just a convenience. For, as you know, the several parts of science have no real boundaries between them.

Welcome to Science in Action.

Jack Myers, Ph.D.
Senior Science Editor
Highlights for Children

Have You Ever Seen a Sleeping Horse?

Horses have their own way
of getting the sleep they need.

Most of us have not seen a sleeping horse. Often I have seen horses standing very quietly, sometimes several side by side. I thought that's how horses might do their sleeping. I was wrong. Horses have their own special way of sleeping.

Scientists have learned how to study sleep in people. Now they are using some of the same methods to study other animals. I found a report by two French scientists on their study of sleep in horses.

Fortunately, there's a way to tell what's going on in an animal even when it's asleep. Muscle and nerve activity always causes small electric currents. And these can be recorded from wire contacts taped at different places on the horse's body surface. The wires lead to a machine that produces a record in the form of a graph. The easiest activity to record is the strong beat of the heart. Contacts against the side of a horse give a graph with a regular spacing of sharp spikes, one for each squeeze of the heart muscle.

Recordings are also made at different places on the head. Those records usually look like wavy lines, some smooth and regular, some jerky with many bumps and wiggles. You might call them brain waves. They tell a little about how active the brain is.

Horse Naps

A horse being studied was kept in a stall, large enough for it to lie down but small enough that a cable of small wires could be kept attached. There was also a TV camera keeping a record of what the horse was doing.

By studying the records and a replay of the videotape, the scientists learned a lot about sleep in horses. They could tell when a horse went to sleep from changes seen in the records. Just as in a sleeping person, most of the muscles relaxed, the heart slowed down, and the brain waves became slower. That is called slow wave, or *SW*, sleep.

And they found periods of the other kind of sleep that also occurs in people. It is called *REM* sleep because of rapid eye movements that happen even though the eyelids

are closed. During REM sleep, the brain waves got faster and the heart and breathing became less regular. Often there were twitchings of the ears and leg muscles. Sometimes the horse even whinnied.

In people, REM sleep is the special time when we do our dreaming. There was no way to tell whether a horse was dreaming, but from its actions it might have been.

In the horses that were studied, REM sleep was about one-fourth of the total sleep time—about the same as in people. And horses sleep mainly at night, as we do. But other characteristics of their sleep were very different. Horses sleep only about three hours a night, and they get that in five or six short naps, each maybe a half hour long.

A horse may drowse when standing up. But in order to relax its muscles and sleep, it needs to be lying down. It has two ways of doing this, which you can see in the illustration. It can stay upright, tuck its front legs underneath, and rest most of its weight on its sternum or breast bone. That's the position in which a horse most often starts its SW sleep.

Later it will roll over partway and lie on its side so that all its muscles can relax. That's when it will have its REM sleep. So a horse does a lot of lying down and getting up during the night.

When a horse is tethered tightly in a narrow stall or when being transported in a trailer, it can't get all the sleep it needs. Then it becomes especially irritable and unpleasant, just as you do when you don't get enough sleep.

Dogs and Cats

If you have a dog or a cat, you may be surprised that horses sleep so little. Dogs and cats often sleep ten or twelve hours a day. In the distant past, when they were wild animals, they were predators. Their hunting trips

often were short. In between, there were long dull periods when they slept.

Horses, cows, and sheep are herbivores. They need to spend a lot of time grazing to get enough grass. And in the wild they were prey animals. It was safer to be awake most of the time and to sleep only in short naps.

Anyway, you can understand why you're not likely to see horses sleeping. They sleep only at night, only lying down, and only in a few short naps.

Kitty Cats and Skydivers

These two falling bodies have a lot in common.

There's an old saying that cats have nine lives. It may come from noticing that cats can have rather long falls without getting hurt much.

Now a scientific study has been made. Two veterinarians in New York City kept track of what happened to 115 cats that had accidentally fallen out of apartment windows. They were big falls, all from more than two stories. For all 115 cats the average fall was five and a half stories, or about eighty-two feet. Many of the cats had injuries, mostly broken bones. The surprising part was that 104 of them survived. And that included a cat that had fallen thirty-two stories!

Falling people are a lot different. Very few people survive a fall of six stories, especially onto a concrete sidewalk. So, what's the cats' secret?

Injuries to an animal come from the force of hitting the ground. And that depends partly on the weight of the animal. You probably weigh about ten times as much as a cat. So, if you and a cat were falling at the same speed, you would hit the ground ten times as hard as the cat.

Air Resistance

The force of hitting the ground also depends on the speed of fall. Because of the steady pull of gravity, a falling body "wants" to go faster and faster the longer it falls. But air gets in its way. You can feel that resistance of air just by putting your hand a little way out of a car window. The faster the car is moving, the harder it is to push air out of the way. For a falling body, air resistance and gravity work against each other.

If an object falls far enough, it reaches a constant speed called its *terminal speed.* Then the force of air resistance holding it up just matches the force of gravity pulling it down. Is there any difference between cats and people in their terminal speed of fall? A big difference. You may weigh ten times as much as a cat, but you have only about five times as much surface. So, air holds back a cat much more than it holds back a person. For a person, the terminal speed is about 120 miles per hour. For a cat, it's only about 60 miles per hour.

There is still one more reason that cats are better at falling. They have a great sense of balance. Even in a short fall they flip their bodies around so that their legs are pointing downward for landing. In falling from a high building, that gives them another advantage. They are spreading out their bodies to get the most effect of air resistance in slowing them down. And they have four legs partly bent and ready to take the force of landing.

Unless they practice at it, people aren't so good at falling. They fall awkwardly, their bodies just tumble, and they don't always land on their feet.

Can people learn to be better at falling? The answer is yes, though not by falling out of tall buildings. They never get to be as quick at it as cats, but people can learn to manage their body position for the best landing possible. Maybe you have seen Olympic divers do acrobatics off a high diving board. They need to enter the water in a good diving position, or they can receive severe injury. You know how much a "belly-slammer" can hurt just from a short dive into a swimming pool.

Some people who have really mastered the art of falling are skydivers. To understand what they do, you first need to think about parachutes. A parachute is a neat invention that works by greatly increasing air resistance. It is like a big twenty-eight-foot umbrella with ropes that attach to a person by a belt and shoulder harness. It is carefully folded into a backpack and can be let out by pulling a cord. Since it takes several seconds to open, a parachute doesn't have time to open during a jump from a tall building. But it works just great for jumping from an airplane. Then the jumper floats down below the parachute at a speed of 10 to 12 miles per hour. Hitting the ground is like jumping off a platform about 4 feet high.

Falling for Fun

Parachutes first came into use as safety devices. They let a pilot bail out and land safely if his plane had an engine failure. In time people tried parachutes just for fun. Then they invented parachuting games, like guiding their chutes to see who could land right on a small target.

Then someone tried falling several thousand feet before opening the parachute. That is how skydiving was born. Now there are clubs of people who skydive for fun. It seems to be rather common to jump from a plane at about 10,000 feet, free-fall down to about 7,500 feet, and then open the chute for a slower ride on down. That gives about a minute of free fall, especially if the skydivers wear baggy suits to help slow them down a little.

Divers learned that by twisting their bodies into different positions they could fall faster or slower or sidewise. So, two divers who jump about the same time can guide themselves together and hold hands. One of the games they play is to see how many divers can come together and hook up to make a pattern of free-falling bodies in the sky.

Now you know a lot about falling bodies, from kitty cats to parachutes to skydivers.

Flashing Fireflies

Here's how they do it.

I think it's great fun to watch fireflies when they are flashing away on a summer evening. If you watch them for a while, you begin to wonder: Why do they do that? And how do they do it?

I thought you might wonder about those questions, too. So I have studied up on fireflies. Here are some of the things I found out.

You may know that our common fireflies are really little beetles and that there are several different kinds of them. The flashes that you usually see a few feet above the ground are made by flying males. A female stays down in the grass. She flashes back when she sees a male flashing overhead. Different kinds of fireflies have small differences in the color of their flashes. Different kinds also may have different lengths of flashes and different lengths of time between flashes. So there is little doubt that the flashes are mating signals. They are used by the males and females of any one kind of firefly to "talk" to each other.

Other Light Makers

The fireflies we see in summer are not the only living organisms that make light. There are many others, especially among the simplest organisms, such as some of the bacteria and fungi and protozoa. One of the world's beautiful sights is the glowing wake behind a ship sometimes seen at night in the warmer parts of the ocean. It is caused by millions of special kinds of protozoa that glow whenever they are bounced around by rough water.

Light from living organisms is so interesting that it has a special name: *bioluminescence*. The way it works is nearly the same—but not exactly the same—in different organisms.

A famous experiment was done just about a hundred years ago. When a firefly tail was ground up in a little water, the gooey mess would glow for several minutes before it became dark.

What could be added to make it glow again? The very best way was to make an extract by boiling up another firefly tail in a little water. The extract would not glow itself. But it would start up a new glow in the gooey mess of the ground-up tail.

That's all it took to get an important idea. There must be some chemical that is used up in making light. The chemical that can be used up came to be called *luciferin,* even though no one knew what kind of chemical it was. There is also something that is not used up in making light but is destroyed by heat. This is a special protein, an enzyme, a piece of chemical machinery that can work over and over again. It is called *luciferase*. In other experiments it was easy to find out that oxygen also is needed.

We have learned a lot more—though not all—about the light-making reaction. Firefly luciferase has been purified. Firefly luciferin has also been purified and even made artificially by chemists. Once that happened, it was easy to show that something else in addition to luciferin was used up in making light. The "something else" turned out to be an energy-carrying chemical that is in all living cells. This is usually called by its initials, *ATP*.

That light-making reaction is now so well known that we can mimic a firefly flash in a test tube. Leave out only one of the things needed. Then squirt that one into the test tube. There will be a flash of light. In doing experiments like that, it was surprising to find how little ATP was needed to get a light flash.

ATP is a very important chemical in all living cells. Like a tiny battery, it is used to store and release energy. Whenever a muscle in your body works, it uses up its ATP. Then it must recharge its ATP before it can work again. You can see that if ATP is so important, then we need a good way to measure it. What's the best way of all? Put some luciferin and luciferase from a firefly in a test tube. Then add a little of whatever you want to test—and measure the amount of light in the flash. That will tell you the amount of ATP. In fact, that's about the most sensitive chemical test I know of. It is used in hospitals and biological research laboratories all over the world.

It is great to think how plain old wondering and curiosity about fireflies has led to such an important, practical result.

What's Your Flash Code?

There are many different kinds or species of fireflies, some-times living together in the same locality. So it's no surprise that each species has its own flash code for communication. Though there are some differences in flash color and length of flashes, the most distinctive feature of a flash code is the timing between flashes.

In the most common North American firefly, the male keeps flying slowly a few feet above the ground, usually at dusk. About every six seconds he makes a half-second flash. After the flash he hovers for about two seconds looking for a replying flash from a female in the grass below. If there is no replying flash in two seconds, he flies forward again and continues his code of a flash every six seconds. The female responds to flashes in that code (even flashes from a small flashlight) and then keeps on flashing as a guide to the male.

In another American species the male signal uses pairs of flashes one second apart and the female's response is a single flash one second after the male's second flash. A species of firefly may be identified by its flash code, which is a built-in behavior pattern.

Talking to Chimpanzees

Can animals learn our language?

There is a question many people have wondered about: How far can we go in teaching some other animal to talk to us in human language? Drs. Allen and Beatrice Gardner are two scientists who set out to answer that question.

The Gardners chose a chimpanzee. Why? Well, for several reasons: it is sociable and imitative, and seems to be an intelligent animal. Chimps are not good at imitating human speech, but they are very good at using their hands. American Sign Language, which is used by deaf people, seemed the best way of trying to talk back and forth between a human and a chimpanzee.

So the Gardners got a baby chimpanzee, about one year old, and named her Washoe. They gave her even more attention than if she had been a human baby. They, or other people, were with her all the time as friends and playmates. While they were with her they talked to each other only in sign language. Their aim was to see how she would learn to talk in human sign language.

Great Imitators

How did they teach her? One way was to take advantage of the well-known tendency of chimps to imitate. You might be interested in this quotation from the article:

> The following is an example of Washoe's delayed imitation. From the beginning of the project she was bathed regularly and according to a standard routine. Also, from her 2nd month with us, she always had dolls to play with. One day, during the 10th month of the project, she bathed one of her dolls in the way we usually bathed her. She filled her little bathtub with water, dunked the doll in the tub, then took it out and dried it with a towel. She has repeated the entire performance, or parts of it, many times since, sometimes also soaping the doll.

Imitation was a help in teaching. Washoe's daily routine included brushing her teeth after every meal. She did not like it at first but got used to it. After many months she learned by herself to make the sign for *toothbrush*—rubbing her front teeth with a finger—when she saw a toothbrush or at the end of a meal.

Before they learn to talk, babies do a lot of babbling, making sounds that do not mean anything. Then when someone repeats to them one of their babbling sounds, it can become a word with meaning. Washoe "babbled" with her hands. By laughing and playing, the Gardners taught her to use one of her own motions to make the sign for *funny*—a finger pressed against her nose.

Sometimes they taught by holding Washoe's hands and moving them just right to make a sign. When she made the sign correctly by herself they rewarded her with something

A sign for *drink*.

she loved—being tickled. She learned the sign for *more*—fingertips brought together—to get more tickling. In time she learned to make the *more* sign to get more food or in games, such as being pushed across the floor in a laundry basket.

By the time she was three years old, Washoe had a "vocabulary" of thirty signs that she could understand and use correctly. And she had even learned to use combinations of signs, such as *please open hurry* and *gimme drink please*.

Washoe and the Gardners learned to talk back and forth to each other in human sign language.

Body-Language Problem

The Washoe experiment was only partly successful. It showed that a human and a chimpanzee could communicate simple ideas to each other. It also raised new questions. In talking, most of us also use some form of "body language"—a smile or a frown or a hand movement. Sign language is based on hand movements. So it was possible that a part of what Washoe learned was in sensing the Gardners' body language rather than in recognizing the signs as symbols.

One way to get around the body-language problem was invented by Duane Rumbaugh. He developed a keyboard with more than a hundred symbols on its keys, each standing for a different word. When a key was pushed, it would light up and also send a message to be recorded by computer. Sue Savage-Rumbaugh has used the keyboard as a means of teaching "words" to a number of chimpanzees.

Sue began with Lana, an adult chimpanzee. To obtain food, Lana was taught to say a sentence on her keyboard, such as *please machine give banana*. After four years Lana was able to use correctly more than a hundred symbols on her keyboard and put them together in sentences. But Sue began to worry whether Lana really understood the meaning of the symbols she was using. Maybe she was just imitating her teacher. Maybe she had just learned that pushing a certain key would give her a banana. Even rats and pigeons can be taught to press a special key to get their food. When Sue turned the conversation around and asked, *please give me banana*, Lana became confused. She could not respond and did not know what to say on her keyboard. Lana had learned to use words without really understanding their meaning. That did not seem like language.

Austin and Sherman

Sue decided on a new direction for her studies. She would use two young chimpanzees, Austin and Sherman, and treat them as if they were preschool children. She would try to teach them to communicate so that each could tell the other something he did not already know. Sue was a patient and skillful teacher. She spent five years teaching them how to use language. Her first problem was to get them to listen to each other. They were not good listeners. They liked action and wanted to talk and interrupt each other rather than listen. To make them listen, Sue invented games that Sherman and Austin could play, first with her and then with each other.

The "final exam" was a hiding game. The game started when Austin went to the refrigerator and watched Sue put banana slices in a box. Then he was encouraged to tell Sherman what was in the closed box. Austin remembered what Sue had put in the box and pushed his key for banana. Then Sherman got into the game. He had not seen what was in the box, but he could see Austin carrying the box and showing on his keyboard the symbol for banana.

The hiding game.

Sherman went to his own keyboard and pushed his key for banana. When both chimps showed the correct food, they got to eat it together. Austin and Sherman took turns in their roles in the game and played it with a perfect score. They both knew that one had information the other needed and that the name of the game was communication.

Curious Kanzi

Even as Sherman and Austin were learning their parts of language, another student came to Sue's school. He was Kanzi, a two-year-old bonobo chimpanzee. Bonobos are a special group, a little smaller in size than the common chimpanzees. They were believed to be more friendly and curious. Naturally Sue wondered if they would be good at learning language skills.

Sue started with a female, Matata, who brought her baby Kanzi to school with her. Matata was not much interested in learning symbols on a keyboard, and Sue was about to stop the project. But then, almost by accident, Kanzi began using the keyboard for words he had learned all by himself just by watching. Four years later Kanzi had a vocabulary of more than a hundred symbols, and could use several together in simple sentences. But his most remarkable accomplishment was that he also learned to understand spoken English. No one had been trying to teach that. He had been listening in on his teachers. It was a surprise to discover that he understood a spoken command almost as well as one given on his keyboard.

Kanzi.

Kanzi became so good at communication that a book about chimpanzee learning has been titled with his name. The book also tells about the other young chimpanzees—almost twelve of them—that have "gone to school." None of them learned to speak. They lack the voice box and the control over lips and tongue that we use in human speech. They have to "speak" the hard way, in sign language or on computer-like keyboards. How good are they at understanding? Sue tested Kanzi and a $2^1/2$-year-old child side by side for their understanding of sentences they had not heard before. They were almost alike in understanding.

The Language Road

Scientists have put a great deal of effort into teaching chimpanzees. What can we say about the result? Can chimpanzees learn to use a human language? Scientists who have studied the question have come to different conclusions.

Linguists, the scientists who study human languages, think that is impossible. They argue that humans use language so well because we have a built-in program for it in our brains. Others argue that the chimps were trained to use words the way other animals can be trained to do tricks. We also ought to consider the conclusion of Sue Savage-Rumbaugh, who has spent more than twenty years with that question. She has said, "Chimpanzees do travel down the language road . . . but they travel more slowly than humans and not as far."

Why Do Snakes Flick Their Tongues?

Snakes lick around to find what they like.

Why do snakes flick their tongues? People have been curious about that question for thousands of years. Many different answers have been suggested. But only recently have scientists learned enough about snakes to get close to an answer.

To people who don't like snakes, the flicking tongue might seem evil. Some people might think it carries poison, but it's easy to show that idea is wrong. Poisonous snakes deliver their venom with special fangs. Most other snakes, even little garter snakes, do a lot of tongue flicking. But none of them has venom on its tongue.

From the way a snake uses its tongue, it seems to be tasting. Taste and smell are two senses that are nice to have, even though you and I don't depend on them very much. We depend more on sight and hearing. But if you lived down among grasses and rocks as a snake does, taste and smell might give you a lot of information about your part of the world.

Can Snakes Taste?

The taste idea looked sensible. But at first a study of snake tongues showed some problems. Scientists discovered that a snake's tongue doesn't have any *taste buds*, the little gadgets packed with nerve endings that give you your sense of taste. Snakes' tongues also lack nerves that could carry taste messages to their brains.

The scientists tried again. They studied the snake's head. It has two cavities, one opening to the mouth and one to the nose. At the back of the nose cavity there is a patch of

cells with nerve connections to the brain. That's where the snake does its smelling.

A different bundle of nerves goes to the brain from two little hollow structures within the roof of the mouth. Each has a little hole to the mouth cavity below. These have come to be called the *vomeronasal* organs. That's where the snake does its tasting.

In one experiment some soot (finely powdered carbon) was spread on the ground where a snake was flicking its tongue. Later the carbon particles were found in the vomeronasal organs. Of course that left the question of how the carbon particles got there.

It was natural to suppose that a snake might taste by slipping the two tips of its tongue into the little holes of the vomeronasal organs. But high-speed movies told a different story. When the tongue flicks out, its two tips move apart before they touch anything. As the tongue is pulled in, the two tips are dragged across little pads on the bottom of the mouth. And then when the snake closes its mouth, those two pads rise up to touch the openings to the vomeronasal organs.

There's a lot we still do not know about the everyday life of a snake. But one of its features is no longer a mystery. By

flicking its tongue, the snake brings back to its vomeronasal organs whatever chemicals are out there. The snake is always tasting its environment.

Tracking Prey

One special use of the snake's tongue is to help it follow the trail of its prey. Scientists have watched carefully to figure out how snakes do it. It's easy to watch garter snakes, which prey on earthworms. For garter snakes, a good trail can be made through a maze of pathways with the slime of earthworms.

Here's the idea we have about why a snake is so good at following a taste trail. It is always pulling back tasty chemicals on the two forks of its tongue. And nerve connections from the vomeronasal organs are always comparing the amount of taste brought in by the right and left fork. Equal amounts of taste on the right and left mean the trail goes straight. More taste on one side means the trail must be turning toward that side. You can say that the snake's forked tongue gives it stereoscopic taste.

Some Lizards Are Tongue Flickers, Too

Lizards and snakes are closely related animals. So it's no surprise that most lizards also flick their tongues. But not all lizards have forked tongues. Geckos, and others that sit and wait for their prey, have only little notches in their tongues, not forks. Monitor lizards, including the big Komodo dragon, use taste trails to go out and find their prey. They are like snakes in having deeply forked tongues.

On the Trail of the Komodo Dragon

This lizard is big enough for a storybook.

Halfway around the world, on Komodo, an island of Indonesia, lives the world's largest lizard. It may grow to be as long as a dining table and as heavy as a grown man. It is sometimes called the Komodo dragon.

The ideas most of us have about dragons come from stories set in olden times. Dragons are pictured as scary animals, maybe shaped like big alligators, breathing fire through mouths full of big teeth.

Thinking about those storybook dragons was enough to make me curious. If there is a real animal out there that someone would call a dragon, what is it like?

Fortunately, there's an answer to that question because a scientist named Walter Auffenberg led a team that spent more than a year studying it. But I should warn you that the Komodo dragon is not a very nice animal, even though it doesn't breathe fire. In some ways, it is completely yucky.

Komodo is a small island, not more than twenty miles across. Together with several neighboring islands, Komodo is home to about five thousand of the big lizards, which are locally called *oras*. Although a few people live in villages there, the whole island is now a national park, and the oras have been protected since 1915.

Big Babies

An ora begins life by cutting itself out of a grapefruit-sized egg. It comes out as a hatchling, almost two feet long. That's longer than most kinds of adult lizards.

By the time it is fully grown, at about twelve years old, it may be eight to ten feet long and weigh more than two hundred pounds. Then it gets to be called a dragon and is not an animal you would like to have in your backyard.

To study oras, scientists set out big funnel-shaped traps made of bamboo and then baited with dead animals. The lizards' noses led them to the traps. (Oras are scavengers, which means that they eat dead animals. Also, they have a keen sense of smell, which they use in finding food.)

The captured oras were weighed and measured. The biggest was more than eight feet long. Some were fitted with a harness holding a little radio. Then the scientists could track the lizards by radio to see where and how they spent their time. And some oras were fitted with electrical thermometers and radios that broadcasted their body

temperatures. Finally, 117 of them were marked with a little spray paint and given names or numbers.

Big Appetites

Although oras eat dead animals when they can, they are also predators. That's no surprise. Most lizards are predators. We don't always think of them that way since they eat little animals, such as insects.

That's what little oras eat, too. But as they grow up, they go for larger animals, like rats and birds. And as adults they often attack large animals, including deer, horses, and water buffalo. Some have even attacked humans.

By watching some of the large oras day after day, the scientists learned that the most common prey were deer. An ora can't catch a deer in a race. Instead it waits in ambush near a trail. Then it rushes out and makes a surprise attack. An ora has big, scary-looking teeth with sawtooth edges. So it can give a very bad bite.

From the way oras hunt live animals and find dead ones, the scientists have no doubt that these lizards depend on their keen sense of smell. They also have long tongues, forked like the tongues of snakes. Like snakes, oras flick out their tongues to touch things. When they find something that might be good to eat, they always check it out by touching it with the tongue.

A Tropical Home

Most big-time predators, like wolves and lions, are "warm-blooded" and have an automatic temperature control like a human's. Their body machinery is always revved up and ready to go. But lizards are "cold-blooded." They need to find ways to manage their body temperature. Before they can go hunting in the morning, oras need to lie in the sun until their bodies warm up.

On most days an ora spends an hour or more basking in the early morning sun. Then it carefully stays in the shade during the afternoon, when it is in danger of getting too warm.

The scientists' records showed that oras are able to keep their body temperature between 95 and 104 degrees Fahrenheit. At night the air temperature often dropped to 80 degrees and sometimes to 76 degrees. Then the lizards found cover in hollow logs, burrows, or other snug places to stay warm.

You can see why the Komodo dragon lives only on Komodo and a few nearby islands. These islands have no other big predators that might compete with oras, and that small part of the world has a steady and cozy temperature. You're not likely to find a Komodo dragon in your backyard.

Flores Sea

Flores

Sumbawa

Komodo

The Ora's range is shown in red.

How to Fuel a Hummingbird

This tiny creature is a fast-food champion.

How to fuel a hummingbird—that may sound like an odd title. Usually we think of fuel as something that makes an engine run, like the gasoline we put in our cars. When it comes to animals, we usually talk about food rather than fuel. But a hummingbird is unusual because it needs so much food to get enough energy. Of all the warm-blooded animals, the hummingbird is the smallest and has the fastest-running body machinery.

The hummingbird gets its food by buzzing around and visiting flowers—lots of them. Hovering above each flower, the hummingbird pokes in its long beak and laps up a drop of sugary nectar with its tongue. It spends a lot of energy to get enough food, and it needs a lot of food to get enough energy. How does it manage?

A team of scientists has completed a study of rufous hummingbirds. Rufous hummingbirds live in the western United States during the summer and then fly about two thousand miles on their migration to a winter home in Mexico.

They made a special feeder, filled with sugar-water, that acted like a gas mask. When a bird was feeding with its mouth and nose inside the feeder, the scientists could measure how fast the bird was using oxygen and how fast it was giving off carbon dioxide. Measurements of the exchange of these two gases have been made on many animals—from insects to elephants. The measurements tell how fast the animal is using energy—how fast its engine is running. And the measurements even tell what kind of food the animal is burning as its fuel. Here's what the scientists found.

A hummingbird had its highest energy rate when it was hovering and feeding, as it usually does at flowers and at feeders. This energy rate was about the same as that of a small flashlight. Since this was the highest energy rate measured, I have shown it as 100 in the table.

Hummingbird Activity	Energy Rate	Fuel Used
Hovering, feeding	100	Sugar
Perched, feeding	70	Sugar
Restrained	25	Fat

When the birds were hovering and feeding, they were burning sugar for fuel. If the bird perched instead of hovering, its energy rate went down to 70. Even at this slower rate, it was still burning sugar.

In a third part of the experiment, the bird was restrained. That meant keeping it quiet in a cloth jacket for about an hour. Then the hummingbird's energy rate went way down to 25. And now it was burning fat.

Like most animals, the hummingbird stores energy, and it does that in two ways. One way is to store energy as a special form of sugar called *glycogen.* Then the energy is stored right in the muscles where it will be used. But there isn't much room in a hummingbird's muscles to store glycogen. It can store only enough glycogen for about five minutes of flying.

The second way that animals store energy, and a way they can store a lot more of it, is to convert the glycogen into fat. Fat makes a better storehouse for energy because it can contain more energy in a smaller space.

The hummingbird, just like other animals, uses fat as its energy reserve—as a car uses a spare gas tank. Even when a hummingbird is restrained, after an hour it has used up its

stored sugar and switched over to fat as its energy reserve. You can see why a hummingbird seems to be so busy, always buzzing around looking for food. It might perch on a twig, but not for long. It can't manage on just three meals a day. It needs another one—right away.

Because of its great need for fuel, a hummingbird has two special problems. One problem comes every night, when the hummingbird can no longer find food. It survives at night by using the same trick many animals use during hibernation—it turns down its energy rate until it is just barely alive. Then every morning the hummingbird turns up its energy rate, warms up again, and begins the search for food.

A second special problem for the hummingbird is its annual migration. It has to fly a long way without many stops for food and rest. To do this, a hummingbird makes special preparations. Late in the summer it works even harder than usual to get more nectar. Then it can convert some of this extra sugar to stored fat. It is building up its energy reserve for the long flight ahead. Throughout its life, a hummingbird rarely stops to rest or take a nap.

Watch a hummingbird, and you will remember the whir of its wings, the flash of its colors, and its skill as an acrobat. Equally spectacular is its way of life—afraid of being hungry, always hurrying to get another meal, a champion of fast-food living.

Nature's Running Machine

The pronghorn antelope is the long-distance champ.

Among animals the champion long-distance runner is the pronghorn antelope. There is a record that one of them was once followed across the prairie for ten minutes at a speed of forty-one miles per hour. Only the cheetah, the hunting cat of Africa, is said to be faster—and that's only for shorter distances.

The pronghorn antelope makes its home on the North American prairie, on the open plains where there is no place to hide. So its safety depends on outrunning predators like wolves. What makes it such a great runner?

When a four-footed animal is running, almost all the energy it spends is used by its leg muscles. So the first question to ask is: How fast can that running machinery work—how fast can it spend energy in running? The best way to answer the question is to measure how fast the animal can use oxygen out of the air that it breathes. That's hard to do for an animal running freely. So the scientists made pets of two orphan antelopes and trained them to run on a treadmill—a wide moving belt. Treadmills are often used by people as exercise machines. Of course a treadmill for an antelope needs to be bigger and faster.

In studying an antelope as a running animal, it helps to have another animal about the same size for comparison. The goat is a natural choice. It is also a plant eater, even looks something like an antelope, and can be trained to run on a treadmill. Experiments on antelopes and goats gave a clear result. An antelope can run a lot faster because it can spend energy five times faster than a goat. If we take the sizes of other animal runners into account, then goats are very much like other animals. It's the antelope that is special.

What's Its Secret?

So what's the antelope's secret? How does its machinery work so much better that it stands out as a champion runner?

The scientists thought about parts of the body machinery especially used in running. Then they asked how well each of these parts works in antelopes and in goats. Here's how their study came out.

An antelope has a larger windpipe and larger lungs. So it can get oxygen to its blood faster. For pumping the blood, it has a larger heart—almost twice as large as the goat's. Its blood has more red cells and hemoglobin, so it can carry a larger load of oxygen to the muscles. It has more muscle tissue, and its muscles have more of the chemical machinery that makes them work. All of those things are needed in running.

The pronghorn antelope is a record runner, but not because of any secret weapon or special invention. Its machinery does all the things that any animal machinery does in running. The antelope's machinery just does it better. Its body seems to be specially designed to be a great running machine.

Here's how scientists discovered how much energy the pronghorns used. When an antelope ran on this treadmill, the gas mask measured how much oxygen the animal took up in breathing. The amount of oxygen was used to calculate how much energy the animal spent.

Champion or Wimp?

You might wonder: Why don't many animals have the special features of body machinery that make the pronghorn antelope such a great runner?

The answer is that the antelope is a specialist. Its body is almost all running machinery. It has very little body fat. That's what other animals use as a reserve to keep them going when food is scarce. So the antelope lives in danger of a cold and icy winter when the prairie grass is covered. And any animal that can spend energy so fast in running probably must spend energy faster even when resting. That means it must work harder to find enough food.

In order to be specialized for running, an antelope's body gives up some of the features that other animals have. This is like saying that an automobile built just for racing is not one you would like to have on a rocky mountain road.

An animal that is a champion in one way is likely to be poorer in other ways. One scientist who thought about this said: "Maybe it's better to be a wimp."

Cheetahs Are Fastest

A track coach proved it.

How fast can animals run? And which is fastest? There are lots of records but also lots of arguments, mainly because there are many problems in measuring the speed of a wild animal.

To time humans, we use carefully measured tracks, runners started by the sound of a gun, and stopwatches. We can be almost as careful in timing horse races, since horses are trained and have riders. But that won't work for wild animals.

Of course there are some ways to compare speeds of different animals. A predator like a cheetah can make a living by running fast to catch up to its prey. And its prey includes fast-running animals like gazelles and antelopes. That's where we got the idea that the cheetah may be the fastest running animal. But how can we measure its speed for the record books?

For some animals, speed has been measured by following the animal in a car while watching the speedometer. Others have been timed by filming the animal as it runs, then using the movie to time how long an animal takes to move its own length. Then it takes a measurement of the animal's length and a little math to figure out its speed. Both of those methods leave some room for argument.

Accurate Measurement

For the cheetah, we now have a measurement of speed done so carefully that it became a scientific experiment. It was done by a British track coach who was visiting in Kenya.

The cheetah in this experiment, Pritchelou, was an orphan that had been brought up on a farm and then returned to the wild. She often came back to the farm, and it was on one of her visits that the measurements were made.

The coach, Mr. N.C.C. Sharp, carefully recorded his experiment. First he measured off a course of 220 yards using a surveyor's tape. That's almost exactly the same length as the 200-meter dash, a distance that sprinters run throughout the world.

The track was on level ground and marked by two posts at each end. At the starting end, Mr. Sharp tied a piece of white wool yarn between the posts. At the finish he marked a line on the ground between the two posts. To make sure his stopwatch was correct, he checked it against two stopwatches of the Kenya Athletic Association. Then he picked a quiet, windless day for the experiment.

To get ready for each test, the cheetah was held 18 yards behind the starting line. A truck, with its engine running and ready to go, was 75 yards down the course.

The coach stood in the back of the truck. In one hand he held the stopwatch, in the other a piece of meat that had been shown to the cheetah. He shouted for the cheetah to be released, and started the stopwatch when she broke the yarn at the starting point.

A driver revved up the truck to stay ahead of the cheetah until well beyond the finish line. The coach stopped the watch when he saw the chest of the cheetah cross the finish line. Then he threw down the meat to let the cheetah eat it.

Two more trials were made, with a thirty-minute rest between them. The times for the three trials were 7.0, 6.9, and 7.2 seconds.

The Cheetah's Time

Mr. Sharp chose the average of 7.0 seconds as the time it took the cheetah to run 220 yards. If you want to do the

Below is the world's fastest known runner—Pritchelou, the cheetah that ran in the experiment. In the photo, she is still a young cheetah. The experiment was done after she became an adult.

math, you can figure that the average speed was 31 yards per second, or 29 meters per second, or 65 miles per hour.

For comparison, a racehorse can run about 41 miles per hour, and champion human sprinters run only about 23 miles per hour.

The design of Mr. Sharp's experiment meant that the cheetah purposely was given a running start. That gives the cheetah a little advantage over other animals, such as race-horses, which are timed from a standing start. But the chee-tah is so much faster that it leaves no doubt that it is the world's fastest running animal.

Of course, like most scientific experiments, this one was not perfect. It did not answer all the questions you might like to ask. A cheetah now holds the record as the word's fastest animal. But we do not know that the cheetah used in the experiment is the world's fasted cheetah.

How the Giraffe Does It

That long neck presents some problems.

Everyone knows that the giraffe looks like a surprising and almost impossible animal. With its long legs and long neck, an adult giraffe may be sixteen feet high. That's tall enough that one could look down at you through a window on the second story of your house.

The details of a giraffe's body—like the arrangement of bones in its skeleton—have been known for a long time.

But some of the details of how its machinery works inside have not been known. One of the interesting questions is how it manages the circulation of its blood.

We know that a giraffe has the same kind of machinery found in many other animals. It has a heart that pumps the blood into tough-walled tubes, the arteries. The larger arteries branch into smaller ones and then into very tiny thin-walled tubes, the capillaries. There are so many capillaries that no cell of the body is very far from the blood carried inside them. Blood passes on through the capillaries and is collected by larger tubes, the veins, which carry it back to the heart.

For the giraffe there seems to be a special problem. Its heart is about eight feet below its head. How does its body pump blood way up to its head with still enough pressure left to squeeze it though the network of tiny capillaries in the brain?

Scientists have wondered about this for a long time. How does the giraffe do it? A team of medical scientists went to Africa to find out. One of them wrote about what they learned in an article in the *Scientific American* magazine. I thought you might like to know about it.

Catching a Giraffe

To study a giraffe in the wild the scientists first had to catch one. They did this with a lasso from a speeding truck out on the plains of Kenya. They tied up the giraffe. On the underside of the neck they gave a local anesthetic so it would not feel the pain of a small operation. The operation was very simple. They just wanted to put a little sensing gadget into the big carotid artery to measure blood pressure near the brain. On the outside they taped on a little transmitter with its batteries. When the experiment was over they caught the giraffe again, took off the gadgets, sewed up the little opening in the skin, and sent him off good as new.

The radio transmitter told about the giraffe's blood pressure, even when the giraffe was a third of a mile away. From this information and other studies, they learned something about how the giraffe does it.

When the giraffe was still lying down after the operation, its neck was at about the same height as its heart. So their measurement was also telling about the pressure of blood coming out of the heart. That is like measuring your blood pressure in your upper arm, at about the same level as your heart. They found that the normal blood pressure of a giraffe is higher than that measured for any other animal. In fact, it turns out that a giraffe's blood pressure is about twice as great as yours.

When the giraffe stood up, the blood pressure in its neck gradually dropped much lower. It seems that the blood pressure at the brain is usually about the same for giraffes and cows and humans. That is interesting because it is important in any animal to keep a good flow of blood through the brain.

The scientific team also learned the answers to some (but not all) of their other questions about how a giraffe's blood supply is managed. They were not surprised to find that in a giraffe the walls of the arteries and heart are thicker than in other animals. These need to be thick in order to stand that very high blood pressure.

So the next time you meet a giraffe you can think about the problem of pumping blood up to its brain. To solve that problem its heart has to work even harder than yours.

A Gigantothermic Puzzle

Leatherback turtles may teach us something about dinosaurs.

Agroup of scientists studying big sea turtles have found some surprising results—so surprising that they may change the way we think about dinosaurs. The scientists were studying leatherbacks, the world's largest turtles. Some of these are more than eight feet long and weigh more than a thousand pounds. They are today's largest living reptiles.

Turtles and other reptiles are cold-blooded. Scientists call them *ectotherms.* Of course they are always spending energy just to stay alive. That means they are making some heat that may warm their bodies a little above the outside temperature. But they can't make extra heat just to stay warm. When it is cold outside, they get cold inside. Then they're sluggish because cold muscles work slowly. When they can, they search for a warm spot. It is common to see lizards basking in the sun to warm up their bodies. Turtles do that, too, by crawling out of the water onto a rock or log in the sun. It's their standard way to rev up their bodies.

Cold-Water Turtles

A reason to study leatherbacks is that they are sometimes found in rather cold waters. In fact, the scientists found some swimming in sea water at 41 degrees F, where most ectothermic animals would be too sluggish even to wiggle. More study showed that their inside deep-down body temperatures were cozy warm, about 83 degrees F. How could they do that?

Other animals, such as mammals and birds, have special ways to keep their bodies warm. Most have a layer of insulation—fur or feathers—to help hold in body heat. And in cold weather they can increase their energy rate to produce more heat. Their bodies can control their temperature. They are *endotherms*. Of course there is a cost in being an endotherm. A warm-blooded animal must consume more food and spend more energy just to keep warm.

In wondering how the big turtles kept warm, the scientists studied them when the turtles were nesting on a beach in Costa Rica. They attached little gadgets like gas masks so they could study the turtles' breathing. Then they measured how fast they were using oxygen. That also measures how fast they were using energy.

The turtles' energy rate was highest when they were working hard at digging and covering their nests. It was only one-fourth of that when they were resting. Then their energy rate was only about half as great as that measured for large warm-blooded mammals. So leatherback turtles are not endotherms. They can keep warm inside just by being so big. They keep their blood flowing mostly deep inside. That lets their skin and outer body layer serve as insulation to keep their inside parts warm.

The leatherbacks are not like most ectotherms, and they are really not endotherms. So the scientists proposed a new name for a class of very large reptiles: *gigantotherms*.

But the scientists' ideas didn't stop with the turtles. Soon they started thinking about dinosaurs. Many dinosaurs were enormous—a lot bigger than any turtle. And no one

Why Big Can Be Better

We should think a little more about this proposal of gigantothermy to see if it is sensible. To do that we need to consider two ideas. The first idea is that the transfer of heat from any body to the air or water around it must go through its surface. When engineers build a gadget to transfer heat—such as an automobile radiator—they purposely design it to have lots of surface. That makes heat transfer easier.

The second idea comes from thinking about the surface of an animal as affected by its size. We will start by doing a "thought experiment." To make it easy we will do it first with blocks. Think of a square block, 2 x 2 x 2 inches. It has six sides, each 2 x 2 inches square. So its surface area is 6 x 2 x 2 = 24 square inches.

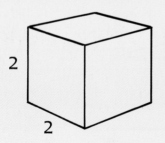
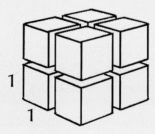

knows for sure if dinosaurs were endotherms or ectotherms.

Dinosaurs had a body plan that's a lot like that of today's reptiles, so some scientists say they were ectotherms. But other scientists ask how dinosaurs could have lived in some of the cold places where their fossils have been found. They think that only a warm-blooded endotherm could have kept warm in such frigid temperatures.

Thanks to this news from leatherbacks, we can think of another possibility. Maybe, like leatherback turtles, the dinosaurs were gigantotherms.

Now suppose we neatly cut that block into eight smaller blocks, each 1 x 1 x 1 inch. Each of these smaller blocks has six sides and each will be 1 x 1 = 1 square inch. So now our total surface is 8 blocks x 6 sides x 1 inch x 1 inch = 48 square inches. We still have the same volume and weight of blocks. But by dividing them to give blocks half as long, we get two times as much surface.

To see how surface changes with size we used square blocks. But this idea has been checked out, and it works for all kinds of shapes (so long as we change only size but not shape). So let's try thinking about turtles. We can think about a one-thousand-pound leatherback turtle, and compare it with one thousand ordinary one-pound turtles you might find in a pond. Those one thousand small turtles would have ten times as much area as that one big leatherback. And their body heat would flow that much faster to the water around them.

Of course we can turn this around and think of what happens as animals get larger. Then there is always a smaller and smaller part of them making up their skin and surface. That's the whole idea of gigantothermy.

BIBLIOGRAPHY

Have You Ever Seen a Sleeping Horse?
Dallaire, A., and Y. Ruckebusch. 1974. Sleep patterns in the pony with observations on partial perceptual deprivation. *Physiology and Behavior* 12:789-796.

Houpt, K.A. 1980. The characteristics of equine sleep. *Equine Practice* 2:8-17.

Kitty Cats and Sky Divers
Whitney, W.O. 1987. High-rise syndrome in cats. *Journal of the American Veterinary Medicine Association* 191:1399-1403.

Flashing Fireflies
Mathews, R.W., and R.R. Mathews. 1978. *Insect Behavior.* New York: John Wiley and Sons, 1978.

McElroy, W.D., and M. DeLuca. 1985. Biochemistry of insect luminescence. *Comprehensive Insect Physiology Biochemistry and Pharmacology* 4:553-563.

Talking to Chimpanzees
Gardner, R.A., and B.T. Gardner. 1969. Teaching sign language to a chimpanzee. *Science* 165:664-672.

Savage-Rumbaugh, S., and R. Lewin. *Kanzi: The Ape at the Brink of the Human Mind.* New York: Wiley/Doubleday, 1994.

Why Do Snakes Flick Their Tongues?
Schwenk, K. 1994. Why snakes have forked tongues. *Science* 263:1573-1577.

On the Trail of the Komodo Dragon
Auffenberg, W. *The Behavioral Ecology of the Komodo Monitor.* Gainesville:University of Florida Press, 1981.

How to Fuel a Hummingbird
Suarez, R.K., J.R.B. Lighton, C.D. Moyes, G.S. Bown, C.L. Gass, and P.W. Hochachka. 1990. Fuel selection in rufous hummingbirds: ecological implications of metabolic biochemistry. *Proceedings of the National Academy of Sciences USA* 87:9207-9210.

Nature's Running Machine
Linstedt, S.L., J.F. Hokanson, D.J. Wells, S.D. Swain, H. Hoppeler, and V. Navarro. 1991. Running energetics of the pronghorn antelope. *Nature* 353:748-750.

Cheetahs Are Fastest
Sharp, N.C.C. 1997. Timed running speed of a cheetah. *Journal of Zoology, London* 241:493-494.

How the Giraffe Does It
Van Citters, R.L., W.S. Kemper, and D.L. Franklin. 1968. Blood flow and pressure in the giraffe carotid artery. *Comparative Biochemistry and Physiology* 24:1035-1042.

Warren, J.V. 1968. The physiology of the giraffe. *Scientific American* 231:96-105.

A Gigantothermic Puzzle
Paladino, F.V., M.P. O'Connor, and J.R. Spotila. 1990. Metabolism of leatherback turtles, gigantothermy, and thermoregulation of dinosaurs. *Nature* 344:858-860.

INDEX